Get Organized Without Losing It

By Janet S. Fox

Edited by Pamela Espeland

Helping kids
help themselves™
since 1983

Library of Congress Cataloging-in-Publication Data
Fox, Janet S.
  Get organized without losing it / by Janet S. Fox ; edited by Pamela Espeland.
    p. cm.
  ISBN-13: 978-1-57542-193-3
  ISBN-10: 1-57542-193-3
  1. Study skills—Handbooks, manuals, etc. 2. Students—Time management—Handbooks,
manuals, etc. 3. Students—Life skills guides. I. Espeland, Pamela. II. Title.
  LB1049.F62 2006
  371.3′0281—dc22

                                                                    2005032809

At the time of this book's publication, all facts and figures cited are the most current
available; all telephone numbers, addresses, and Web site URLs are accurate and active;
all publications, organizations, Web sites, and other resources exist as described in this
book; and all have been verified. The author and Free Spirit Publishing make no war-
ranty or guarantee concerning the information and materials given out by organizations
or content found at Web sites, and we are not responsible for any changes that occur
after this book's publication. If you find an error or believe that a resource listed here
is not as described, please contact Free Spirit Publishing. Parents, teachers, and other
adults: We strongly urge you to monitor children's use of the Internet.

Cover and interior design by Marieka Heinlen
Illustrations by Mike Gordon

10 9 8 7 6 5 4 3 2 1
Printed in the United States of America

Free Spirit Publishing Inc.
217 Fifth Avenue North, Suite 200
Minneapolis, MN 55401-1299
(612) 338-2068
help4kids@freespirit.com
www.freespirit.com

Free Spirit Publishing is a member of the
Green Press Initiative, and we're committed
to printing our books on recycled paper
containing a minimum of 30% post-
consumer waste (PCW). For every ton
of books printed on 30% PCW recycled
paper, we save 5.1 trees, 2,100 gallons of
water, 114 gallons of oil, 18 pounds of air
pollution, 1,230 kilowatt hours of energy,
and .9 cubic yards of landfill space. At
Free Spirit it's our goal to nurture not only
young people, but nature too!

Printed on recycled paper
including 30%
post-consumer waste

green
press
INITIATIVE

Dedication

For Jeff and Kevin: With you by my side, I'm never lost.

And for Barbara, my mom, who also loved words.

Acknowledgments

Special thanks to Kathy Whitehead and Shirley Hoskins; to Jane Beatty; to Dudley, BJ, and June; and to my students and colleagues at St. Michael's. Your guidance and support are invaluable.

My thanks to Larry Rand, who taught me in ninth grade how to get organized.

Thank you to my editors, Trina Wentzel, and the exceptional Pamela Espeland. To Mike Gordon for his wonderful illustrations. And to Judy Galbraith, Marjorie Lisovskis, and all at Free Spirit who recognize that kids need loving guidance.

Contents

Quick Quiz

2. Do you spend tons of time looking for things you need to do your schoolwork or homework?

9. Do you feel like you're always running behind?

1. Is your desk at school a disaster?

6. Is your school locker a shocker?

7. Is your backpack a black hole*?

4. Would your head fall off if it weren't fastened on?

10. Have you ever missed out on fun because your schoolwork didn't get done?

5. Are you forever losing the stuff you need to do your schoolwork or homework?

3. Do you wish you were more organized?

8. Are the questions on this quiz in the right order?

* **Black hole:** A place in space where everything gets sucked in and disappears.

If you answered **YES** to one or more of the questions on the quiz, keep reading. Help is on the way.

If you answered **NO** to question 8, terrific! You can tell when things are organized—and when they're not.

Hey, that's a start.

Picture This

You plop down in your seat at school seconds before the bell rings. The teacher announces a pop quiz, and you search high and low for a pencil. When you finally find one, it needs sharpening, but there's no time.

During the quiz, you change your mind about the answer to question #3. But the eraser on your pencil is flat, and you rub a big black smudge on the paper. You waste time trying to fix it. When the teacher calls "Time's up!" you're still not finished with the quiz.

Then the teacher asks for yesterday's homework. You dig through your backpack, which is crammed with crumpled papers—everything but your homework.

Is it still on the kitchen table at home? Or maybe under your bed? You can't remember, and it's too late anyway. No homework means another zero.

When you get home after soccer, you watch TV for a while. Then you eat dinner, help with the dishes, and play with the dog.

About an hour before bedtime, you go into your room and dump the contents of your backpack on the floor. You realize you forgot your science book. Oh, no! There's a test tomorrow! At least you've got your class notes....

You reach for your binder, which is so overstuffed that it pops open and papers fly everywhere. Your science notes—when you finally find them—are a major mess.

You try to study for the test, but what's the use? You give up and go to bed, but you're way too worried to sleep.

The bad news is—you probably won't do well on the test. The good news is—things don't have to be this way.

By the time the next test comes around, you can be a new person. Someone who's calm. Someone who's organized. Someone who's ready to do your best work.

TIP: Being organized does **not** mean being a total neat freak. It means spending **less** time going crazy and **more** time having fun.

Basic Tools for Getting Organized

To get organized, you don't need fancy furniture or a PDA (personal digital assistant). You don't need special computer software or an MP3 player with built-in calendars.

You don't even need a parent who says, "Do your homework!" "What died in your backpack?" or "You're going to miss the bus AGAIN!"

What you **do** need are some basic tools. Let's start with things that will get you **to and from** school.

A backpack with at least two compartments. Keep your everyday going-to-school stuff—house keys, wallet, calculator, folding umbrella—in the smaller compartment(s). Use the larger one(s) for your binder and books.

A clear plastic pouch for storing small items that usually get lost in the bottom of your pack. You can use a pencil pouch, a makeup pouch, or a heavy food storage bag with a zip top.

Some schools have rules about backpacks.
Like: No solid backpacks—mesh or see-
through only. No rolling backpacks—they
can be a tripping hazard. (Rolling backpacks lighten the load for many kids, but
some schools still won't allow them. Or
they allow them but make kids carry them
inside the school building...which kind of
misses the whole point.) To make sure you
don't get the wrong kind of backpack, check
with your teacher before you buy.

The Curse of the Too-Heavy Backpack

Does your backpack weigh almost as much as you do?

Thousands of kids are injured each year because of overloaded backpacks. Experts say that your backpack should weigh no more than 10 percent of your weight. In other words, if you weigh 90 pounds, your backpack should weigh 9 pounds. Not empty...**full.**

Some kids carry backpacks that weigh as much as 45 pounds! No wonder they have back pain, neck pain, or shoulder pain. Sometimes this causes kids to miss out on school or sports activities.

So travel as light as you can. Carry only what you really need. Don't load up on personal items. And even if it looks cool to sling your backpack over one shoulder, don't. Wear it like it's made to be worn: on your back, using both straps.

Adjust the straps so the weight of the backpack hangs in the middle of your back, where your muscles are strongest. If your backpack has a waist strap, use it.

TIP: For many kids, the heaviest things in their backpacks are their textbooks. If lugging textbooks to and from home is a problem for you, start by bringing home only the books you need for that night's homework (or that weekend's study). No science assignment? Leave the science textbook in your locker.

If you're still loaded down with textbooks, talk with your teacher. The school may be able to loan you an extra set to keep at home for the year.

A homework folder. This is any folder with two pockets. The pocket on the **left** is for homework you need to do. Label it "Home." The pocket on the **right** is for homework you've done. Label it "School."

You can make a homework folder using heavy paper and tape or staples.

A pocket folder. You'll use this to hold clean writing paper. If you just throw paper in your backpack, it will end up looking like the wrapper from your sandwich.

A large sheet of colorful construction paper folded in half and stapled along the sides makes a great pocket folder.

A really good binder. The best ones have a locking ring mechanism—the kind that snaps open and closed. If (make that **when**) you drop your binder, everything won't fall out.

What **size** binder is best? One with 1½" or 2" rings. That should be enough to hold 5 school subjects.

Some binders have a clear plastic cover sleeve. You might use it to hold an assignment sheet or your homework checklist (more about that later). That way, you'll be sure to see it.

Some schools have rules about binders. Like: No giant three-ring binders. They're too big to fit in many desks and too heavy to carry unless you're an Olympic weightlifter.

Things to keep your binder organized. Like:

- **Subject dividers.** Colorful subject dividers make it easier to find things in your binder. Be sure to label the tabs by subject: English, Science, History, Math, Geography…. You can even divide subjects into sections. In English, you might want separate tabs for Vocabulary, Spelling, and Writing. **TIP:** You might add a Personal Reference Section tab. Keep spelling demons, math facts, science facts, how-to lists, and other helpful study tools there.

- **A zippered pencil pouch.** Your pouch should be big enough to hold 2–3 sharpened pencils, an eraser, and a short ruler. It should have a pre-punched edge that fits the rings of your binder.

- **Sheet protectors.** These clear plastic sleeves protect important handouts and other papers from smudges, spills, and tears. If your teacher gives you a handout listing all of the math assignments for the year, put it in a sheet protector. If you spend hours coloring in the countries on a map of the world, put it in a sheet protector.

- **Two-pocket, three-hole-punched folders.** Sometimes you have a stack of handouts you need to keep together. These folders do the job. Like subject dividers, they come in colors. **TIP:** To be super-organized, you can color-coordinate your folders with your subject dividers.

- **A portable three-hole punch.** This is handy for times when your teacher is too busy to punch a handout for you.

You also need some basic tools to keep it together **in** school. Like:

A small box to hold pencils, erasers, and other small items. Many stores sell standard plastic school-supply boxes.

You can decorate a small cardboard box you find at home, but check first that it fits in your desk at school and holds everything you need.

Things to go in the box. These are the school supplies that most students need. Check with your teacher to find out if you should have anything else.

- 4 or 5 sharpened pencils with good erasers
- rubber eraser
- small pencil sharpener
- scissors
- small ruler
- small bottle of glue or glue stick
- roll of tape
- paper clips
- small stapler
- highlighters
- colored pencils

Make a copy of the shopping list on pages 20–21. Check off the things you already have. The extra lines are for writing other things you may need. (There are a few things on this list we haven't talked about yet, but be patient—we will.)

Show the list to a parent or other family grown-up and ask for help getting your supplies. Bring the list to your local discount store or office supplies store. Many grocery and drug stores also sell these items.

If you can't get everything at once, work your way down the list.

My Get-Organized Shopping List

- [ ] Backpack with at least two compartments
- [ ] Clear plastic pouch
- [ ] Homework folder
- [ ] Pocket folder
- [ ] 1½" to 2" three-ring binder
- [ ] Subject dividers
- [ ] Zippered pencil pouch
- [ ] Sheet protectors
- [ ] Two-pocket, three-hole-punched folders

- [ ] Scissors
- [ ] Small ruler
- [ ] Small bottle of glue or glue stick
- [ ] Roll of tape
- [ ] Paper clips
- [ ] Small stapler
- [ ] Highlighters
- [ ] Colored pencils
- [ ] Locker shelves

- ☐ Portable three-hole punch
- ☐ Small box for small items
- ☐ About 10 sharpened pencils (some for your pencil pouch, some for your supplies box)
- ☐ Two rubber erasers (one for your pouch, one for your box)
- ☐ Two small pencil sharpeners (one for your pouch, one for your box)

- ☐ Magnetic hooks
- ☐ Magnetic file pockets
- ☐ Plastic stacking drawers
- ☐ Student planner
- ☐ _____
- ☐ _____
- ☐ _____
- ☐ _____
- ☐ _____

Desk Disasters, Locker Shockers, and Other Major Messes

Which of these statements is true for you?

1. My desk at school and locker are neat and tidy. There's a place for everything. I can always find what I need.

2. My desk and locker are kind of messy. I can usually find what I need, but it might take a while.

3. My desk is a disaster and my locker is a shocker.

If you picked **#1,** you can probably skip this part of the book. Take a bike ride, listen to music, read a book, call a friend, or go invent something.

Did you pick **#2** or **#3?** Stay put and keep reading.

How to Survive a Desk Disaster

Your desk is not a wastebasket. It's easy to toss that used tissue into your desk (ewww!), but it's better to toss it into the trash.

Your desk is not a homework folder. Stuff homework into your desk and you might as well feed it to the dog. Use your homework folder instead.

Your desk is not a refrigerator. Don't use your desk to store food, which you'll probably forget about until it rots and smells horrible and grows mold.

Let's start with a **clean-up.** Go through your desk as soon as you can. Toss the trash. Put important papers where they belong—in your binder or your homework folder.

Some teachers allow time for a weekly classroom clean-up. If that doesn't happen in your classroom, plan to take a few minutes on your own. Friday is a good day to tackle this task. That way, when you return to school on Monday morning, you'll find a nice, clean desk waiting for you.

Try not to fall over from the surprise.

Q: Some people say that a messy desk is a sign of a **creative** mind. Others say that a messy desk is a sign of a **cluttered** mind. Still others say that a clean desk means you're a neat freak. Who's right and who's wrong?

A: Who cares? What matters is what works for you. But for most people, a messy desk is a big time-waster.

How to Handle a Locker Shocker

NEWS FLASH!
Student Opens Locker Door,
Is Crushed To Death By Falling Objects

NEWS BULLETIN!
Student Opens Locker Door,
Faints From Awful Stink Of Ancient Gym Clothes

NEWS CRAWL!
Student Spends Years Searching Locker For
Permission Slip, Misses Field Trip, Doesn't Graduate

Get the message? Like your desk, your locker is not a wastebasket, a homework folder, or a refrigerator. Plus it's not a dirty clothes bin, a dumpster, or one of those self-storage places people rent to hold all the stuff that won't fit in their garage.

Your locker is where you put your coat or jacket, books, supplies, and other items while you're in class. It's where you store stuff you'll need to find during the school day.

Some schools have rules about kids carrying backpacks during the school day. It's okay to carry your backpack to and from school, but once you arrive at school, away it goes—in your locker.

Let's start with a **clean-up** here, too. Get rid of anything that doesn't belong. Not sure if that hard, shriveled-up orange stick is a crayon or a carrot from last month's lunch? **When in doubt, throw it out.**

Do you need extra help organizing what **does** belong in your locker? Many students find these locker tools useful:

- locker shelves

- magnetic hooks

- magnetic file pockets

- plastic stacking drawers

These are included on the shopping list on pages 20–21.

> **Some schools have rules about locker tools.** Check first to find out what's allowed at your school.

Pssst...

Sometimes a messy desk or locker doesn't mean you're a slob. It means there are other things going on in your life, and you just can't handle being organized right now.

Maybe you're having trouble paying attention or listening in school. Maybe you don't understand the directions the teacher gives you. Maybe you can't see the board or you can't read the teacher's handwriting.

Maybe you're so far behind with your schoolwork that you think you'll never catch up. Maybe school is so boring for you that you just don't care. Or maybe things are happening at home that make it hard for you to focus on school.

TIP: If a messy desk or locker is the least of your worries, talk to an adult you trust. Start with a parent, another family grown-up, or a teacher you like. If your school has a counselor, talk with him or her. School counselors can be good listeners.

How to Manage Other Major Messes

Once you've tackled your desk and your locker, cleaning out your backpack and binder will be a breeze.

Best of all, you can do this at home. You don't have to organize your personal things at school, where time is crunched and your teachers and class-mates are nearby. Why let them in on your dirty little secrets, er, gym socks?

Start with your **backpack**—the place most likely to be a biohazard.*

1. First, clear your room of curious family pets and small children. (It's for their own safety.)

2. Next, turn your backpack upside-down and dump its contents on the floor. Shake it to make sure even the stickiest, most stubborn items fall out.

3. Now sort the debris. Go through loose papers and put them where they belong—in your handy homework folder, or your binder. Sharpen loose pencils and put them back in your pencil pouch. Put gross, smelly clothes in the laundry.

4. If anything in the debris pile tries to crawl away, hit it with your shoe or save it for a science project.

* **Biohazard:** Something that is very bad for you and the environment. Like a year-old tuna sandwich.

Backpack neat and tidy? Move on to your **binder.** No problem—you're an expert who knows the routine. Sort, trash, put things where they belong.

Give yourself a high-five when you're done. You've accomplished a lot. Nothing will ever be this hard again—unless you slide back into your old ways. Which you won't, if you form the checkup habit.

Give Yourself Regular Checkups

Open wide and say **aaahhhhh.**

1. Each day, before you start your homework, take everything out of your backpack. Sort, trash, put things where they belong.

2. Each week, clean out your desk and locker.

3. Every week or two, check your school supply box. Take it home and ask a parent or other family adult to help you freshen it up.

4. Every couple of weeks, go through your binder. Throw away anything you know you don't need or want anymore. Keep older handouts, quizzes, and tests safely at home, in case you need them at some point in the future. If you're not sure what to do with some of your papers, ask a parent or other family adult for advice.

Plan for
School Success

You've cleaned out your desk, your locker, your backpack, and your binder.* Everything is where it belongs. You can find what you need when you need it.

You're ready to make a plan for school success. For this, you'll need a few new tools and strategies.

---

* You **have** cleaned them out, right?

Use a Student Planner

To make a plan, you need (duh) a **planner.**

There are about a zillion different student planners to choose from. Visit an office supplies store and look around. Or go online, search for "student planners," and click on a few links.

Some Web sites have planner templates (forms) you can download, print out, and start using right away. Ask your teacher or media specialist for help finding these. You can even create your own forms.

There are many different types of student planners.

- **Monthly view** planners show a whole month on two pages. (Not much writing room there.)

- **Weekly view** planners show one week on two pages. This is the size that most students use.

- **Two-page-per-day** planners are great if you also like to use your planner as a journal or daily diary.

Some planners just have the days and dates, with blank lines or spaces for writing. Some look more like assignment notebooks, with subject names and boxes to check when you finish each assignment.

Some have places to write lists of things to take home and bring to school, weekly goals, long-term projects, teacher and parent messages, and more.

Some schools provide students with planners. Often, these have the school logo on the cover and a special section with school handbook pages, schedules, and maps. If your school gives you a planner, that's the one you should use.

Jefferson School

9 Great Reasons to Use a Student Planner

1. **A planner is portable.** You can carry yours to and from school in your backpack.

2. **A planner never forgets.** Unlike the human head, it has no holes in it, so things can't fall out.

3. **A planner prevents scheduling problems.** Did a friend invite you to go skating two Saturdays from now? Check your planner before saying yes. Uh-oh, that's the day of the track meet!

4. **A planner keeps all of your important information in one place.** No more paper scraps, sticky notes, or inky, smeared reminders written on your hand.

5. **A planner reminds you of what you need to do and when.** You will no longer need parents, teachers, or other adults in your life. (Just kidding.)

6. **A planner helps you keep track of important projects.** Write down everything you need to do, and you're less likely to forget a task or a due date.

7. **A planner helps you reach your goals.** Break down a big goal into smaller steps, write each step in your planner, finish one step at a time, and before you know it, you're there.

8. **A planner can be whatever you want it to be.** Yours might be a simple list of homework assignments, school projects, and activities. Or it might include your address book, lists of books you want to read and movies you want to see, your daily journal, notes about ideas you have, your hopes and dreams.... What else? It's up to you.

9. **A planner frees up valuable space in your brain.** When you write down many things you need to remember, you don't actually need to remember them. You just need to remember **one** thing: to look in your planner.

Try these planner tips and tricks:

- If you're extra busy with homework and activities, use a **daily planner.** If you're not so busy, use a **weekly planner.**

- When you first get your planner, spend time checking it out. Decide how you'll use it. Where will you write long-term assignments? After-school activities? How will you keep track of your goals so you're sure to reach them? **Personalize** your planner. Make it your own.

- Write in your planner in **pencil,** not ink. That way, when things change, you can erase them instead of crossing them out.

- Mark really important events and due dates with a **highlighter** or **stick-on stars.**

- Use **highlighters** or **colored pencils** for different subjects or types of activities.

- Remember that all work and no play makes life dull, dull, dull...*zzzzzzzzzzz*. Be sure to **leave room for fun times,** relaxing times, and special times with friends and family. Write those in your planner, too.

- Check your planner **first thing every morning.** You'll know what the day will bring.

- Check your planner **last thing every night.** You'll go to sleep feeling ready for tomorrow.

Plan to Manage Your Time

A planner helps you see what's happening in your life. Let's look now at how to prevent **event overload.**

Your time at school is already organized. School starts and ends at the same time each day. Lunch happens at the same time. You know when you'll be in science, in math, and in homeroom.

Some of your time outside of school is probably organized, too. You may have sports, scouts, music lessons, and other places you have to be during the week.

Are you a good time manager? Do you spend your time wisely or waste it? You'll probably waste a lot **less** time now that you've cleaned out your desk, locker, backpack, and binder, because you won't be searching high and low for your stuff.* You need to manage **time** just as well as you're now managing **space.**

* It would also help if you cleaned your **room,** but that's a topic for another book.

On a sheet of lined paper, make a list of the things you usually do after school on a normal weekday. Your list might look something like this:

Activity	Estimated Time	Actual Time
Go to swim team practice		
Chill out at home		
Have a snack		
Watch TV		
Play a video game		
IM my friends		
Get ready for homework		
Set the table for dinner		
Eat dinner		
Help clean up after dinner		
Watch TV		
Do homework		
Play on the computer		
Get ready for bed		

Once you've made your list, **estimate** how much time you spend on each thing. Write your estimates on your list.

Activity	Estimated Time	Actual Time
Go to swim team practice	45 minutes	
Chill out at home	10 minutes	
Have a snack	5 minutes	
Watch TV	20 minutes	
Play a video game	10 minutes	
IM my friends	15 minutes	
Get ready for homework	5 minutes	
Set the table for dinner	5 minutes	
Eat dinner	20 minutes	
Help clean up after dinner	20 minutes	
Watch TV	30 minutes	
Do homework	60 minutes	
Play on the computer	10 minutes	
Get ready for bed	10 minutes	

The next school day, record the **real** times you spend on each thing. Compare the real times with the estimates.

What do you see?

That you watch more TV than you thought? That you play on the computer for two hours but do homework for only ten minutes?

How could you make better use of your time? You'll need a parent or other family adult to help you figure out the answer to this question.

Make a copy of the After-School Scheduler on pages 50–51. Sit down with the adult and fill in your chores, responsibilities, and activities for a typical week. Lightly color in those blocks with colored pencil.

Time	Monday	Tuesday	Wednesday	Thursday	Friday
2:30–3:00	Travel to home, after-school activities				
3:00–3:30	Piano lessons	Volleyball practice		Volleyball practice	
3:30–4:00	Travel				

The blank places on the chart show how much time you have for homework and studying, plus your free time. Now you can plan your homework and study time **first,** and **then** your free time.*

* Not the other way around.

After-School Scheduler

Time	Monday	Tuesday	Wednesday	Thursday	Friday
2:30–3:00	Travel to home, after-school activities				
3:00–3:30					
3:30–4:00					
4:00–4:30					
4:30–5:00					
5:00–5:30					
5:30–6:00					

6:00–6:30				
6:30–7:00				
7:00–7:30				
7:30–8:00				
8:00–8:30				
8:30–9:00				

Ready for school, ready for bed, get a good night's sleep!

Plan for Homework

Now that you can see your homework and study time, here's how to make the most of it.

Use a homework checklist. See pages 54–55 for a checklist you can copy and use. Staple or clip it to the front of your homework folder, or slip it into the clear plastic sleeve of your binder. Start each week with a fresh copy.

Leave your homework folder on top of your desk. Use the checklist to remind yourself of what you need to take home that day in order to do your homework. Ask your teacher to look at your list at the end of the day.

Homework Time

Have a regular homework time. Some kids get their homework done right after school. Other kids run off steam first and then do their homework. What works best for you?

Talk it over with your parents or other family adults. Then decide on a regular homework time—a set time when you'll do your homework every day. On some days, you may have to adjust around other appointments or commitments, but you'll work best if you stick close to the same time each day.

TIP: Even when you don't have homework, use your homework time to learn. Read a book, study your math facts or spelling words, or work on a long-term project.

Homework Checklist

I need these things to do my homework	Monday	Tuesday	Wednesday	Thursday	Friday
Planner					
Filled out					
Checked by teacher					
Textbooks					
Workbooks					
Worksheets/handouts					
Notebooks					

Special notes, permissions, forms to be signed by parent/caregiver					
(What else?)					
(What else?)					
(What else?)					

Q: How much time each day should I spend on homework?

A: About 10 minutes per grade. In other words, if you're in third grade, you should spend about 30 minutes each day on homework. In fourth grade, about 40 minutes. In sixth grade, about an hour. If you're in grade 730, plan to spend 7,300 minutes every day doing homework.

But seriously: If you regularly spend hours and hours and hours doing homework, ask a parent or other family adult to talk with your teacher. Life is more than homework.

Have a regular homework place. One day you do your homework at the kitchen table, the next on the living room floor, the day after in the bathtub while singing along with your favorite band....

Sorry, that won't cut it. If possible, you want to do your homework in the same place every day. Someplace quiet where you can work without being bothered or distracted.

If you have a desk or table in your room, and if you have your own room, great. If not, ask a parent or other family grown-up to help you find a regular quiet study space.

These are the things you'll need in your homework space, wherever it is:

- **A comfortable chair that supports your lower back.** It's fine to read a story sprawled on a sofa or beanbag chair, but for homework, you should sit up fairly straight. Your chair should also be the right height so you can keep both feet on the floor and work without hunching over.

- **A strong light.** A bright light overhead is good. A desk lamp over your shoulder is better.

- **Study supplies** like the ones you keep at school (paper, pencils, sharpener, eraser, scissors, ruler, glue, tape, paper clips, stapler, staples, highlighters, colored pencils) and a few more (calculator, markers). Store these in a plastic box so you can put them out of the way when you're finished working.

- **A dictionary, a thesaurus, and maybe an atlas and an almanac.** Over time, try to collect a small set of reference books.

- **A small erasable white board and dry-erase markers** for doing things you'd normally do on scratch paper (like figuring out answers to math problems). Or you can use it to list all of the homework you need to do that day. As you finish each assignment, erase it from the board.

- **A big plastic file box, large binder, or stacking plastic drawers.** Store class notes, handouts, old quizzes, and other papers you don't need for the moment. At the end of the school year, you'll have a history of what you did and a handy reference for any final tests.

- **A wastebasket.** A paper grocery bag works well, too, as long as you don't toss half-empty juice boxes into it.

Q: Which home- work assignments should I do first? The easiest or the hardest?

A: That depends. Sometimes it's nice to get the easy things out of the way first (the spelling list, the math worksheet) and then tackle the tough ones (the history project). Sometimes doing a hard assign- ment first makes everything else seem like a piece of cake. You can decide each day how you feel. Number each assignment on the white board or in your planner in the order in which you'll do it.

Use a task timeline. A task timeline breaks any assignment into smaller pieces—and puts you in control of your time. It helps you pace yourself so you don't rush through an assignment or take all night to do it.

A task timeline might look like this:

Write a Paragraph About Cats		
Planning ⟶	Working ⟶	Checking
5 minutes	10 minutes	5 minutes

Your timeline shows that you'll spend 5 minutes organizing your ideas for the paragraph (planning), 10 minutes writing (working), and 5 minutes proof-reading and correcting (checking).

For a math assignment, you could use your planning time to estimate the answers to math problems.

You can write your task timelines on scrap paper—or on your white board.

Deal with Distractions

These days, it seems, most kids **multi-task.** They talk on cell phones, IM their friends, watch TV, play computer games, read email, and listen to tunes while studying the words for tomorrow's spelling test.

Hey, if they can do this and still do well in school, good for them.

Not everyone can study and learn with distractions. In fact, most kids do much better with **quiet.** If that includes you, try these tips.

- Turn off the TV, the radio, the boom box, the MP3 player, and the computer (unless you're using it for research). Set your chat or IM status to "away." Now it's just you and your homework. Guess you'd better get it done.

- Ask your siblings not to bug you while you're doing your homework. If they bug you anyway, go to a parent or other family grown-up for help.

- Make a "Do Not Disturb" sign to hang on your door—or to put on the kitchen table, if that's your regular homework place.

- When random thoughts invade your brain ("I wonder if he/she likes me… What was that mystery meat I had for lunch today…"), don't try to block them. Instead, write them down on a note pad or scrap paper. Then set it aside.

- If your homework place is noisy, try listening to soft music through headphones. Instrumental music (music without words) is less distracting.

If you've tried everything and you still can't study, maybe you're tired, hungry, or bored. Take a short nap, eat a healthy snack, or shoot some hoops. The homework will still be there when you return.

Homework is like that—it won't go away.

Plan to Be Ready for School Each Day

Is your morning a **blur** of getting dressed, gulping breakfast, and dashing out the door?

Do you often **forget** things you're supposed to bring to school?

Are you already **stressed out** by the time you get to school?

That's no way to start your day. So don't.

Pick your clothes the night before. The five minutes before you rush to catch the bus or car pool is not the time to decide if the striped shirt goes with the plaid pants. (**Hint:** It probably doesn't.) Hang your clothes front and center in your closet or drape them over a chair in your room. And try not to change your mind in the morning.

If you wear a school uniform, you're lucky. Even if you do think it's dorky. A school uniform means you have one less decision to make at night before you go to bed.

Pack your lunch the night before. If it's your job to pack your own lunch for school, do it before you go to bed at night. You might have the kitchen all to yourself and get first dibs on the best apple.

Try to pack a healthy lunch. You'll have more energy for the afternoon. Avoid fried snacks, cookies, candy, white bread, and soda. Give trail mix, air-popped popcorn, turkey on whole-grain bread, and real fruit juice or water a chance. If you're in the habit of packing junky lunches, ask a parent or other family adult to help you do a meal makeover.

TIP: If you don't bring your lunch to school, be sure to put tomorrow's lunch money or milk money where you won't forget it. Put it in your shoe, or in the plastic pouch in your backpack.

Is That Your Lunch Box or a Garbage Can?

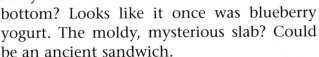

What's that mushy brown thing? Must be last week's half-eaten banana. And the carton with the slimy stuff at the bottom? Looks like it once was blueberry yogurt. The moldy, mysterious slab? Could be an ancient sandwich.

Would you eat out of a garbage can? Probably not. So don't treat your lunch box like one (or your thermal lunch bag, if that's what you use). Bring it home from school every night and clean it out. Throw away perishables. Put the uneaten orange back in the fridge. Wash reusable containers in hot, soapy water. Then wash and dry your lunch box, too. You'll have a clean, fresh place to put tomorrow's yummy lunch.

Plan your breakfast the night before. Breakfast is the most important meal of the day. It's a fact: Kids who eat breakfast do better in school. So don't skip breakfast—and don't just stuff your face with sugary cereal or toaster waffles swimming in sticky syrup. Try some whole-grain toast or cereal, an egg, fruit, and a glass of orange juice.

Pile everything you need next to the door you use when you leave for school. Put your coat, hat, boots, backpack, binder, gloves, school project, and gym clothes—anything you don't want to forget the next day—right where you'll be sure to see them.

TIP: When you make time each night to get ready for school, you start the next day feeling calm and in control. You're more relaxed when you get to school because you know you have everything you need.

Plan for Long-Term Projects

Many students dread long-term projects. But their parents dread them even more.

Kid: Mom, can you take me to the library tonight?

Mom: The library is closed tonight. Why?

Kid: I have a history project.

Mom: What kind of history project?

Kid: A report on the Civil War. We're supposed to read a book and write a paper and draw a map and build a three-dimensional battlefield model and make a soldier's costume.

Mom: All that? Wow. And when is this project due?

Kid: Tomorrow. Can you help?

Life is easier for you and your parents when you get long-term projects done on time. Here's how.

1. Start early. Don't wait until the last minute.

2. Write the project due
date in your student
planner. Write it in
red, or circle it in red,
or draw flowers or
stars or arrows around
it—anything to make
it stand out.

3. Make a list of all the
things you need to do for the project. Don't
worry about the order at first. Just list everything. You're breaking down the project into
baby steps—the trick to getting it done.

4. Decide what steps you'll do first, second, and so on. Number your list.

5. Make a copy of the Long-Term Project Planner on pages 76–77. Write down the steps you need to complete and when you need to complete them. Use the spaces on the calendar part of the Project Planner to describe what you will do each day—your tasks for that day.

   You'll find an example of a filled-in Project Planner on pages 78–79.

6. Write each day's tasks in your student planner. Then you can see how and where they fit in with your other responsibilities.

7. Figure out how much time you'll need to do each task. Write the times in your student planner.

   Example: You estimate that it will take you 2 hours to search the library for books you need. You add that time to your homework schedule for Tuesday and Wednesday.

TIP: Always give yourself **more time** than you think you'll really need. That way, when you finish early, you'll have plenty of time to celebrate—or relax.

8. Stick to your plan. If you miss a day, get back to work the next day.

9. See step #1.

Don't procrastinate! Focus on each baby step toward your goal. Take little breaks between steps. Keep doing the steps and your project will get done.

The first time or two you plan a long-term project, it might seem like a lot to sort out. Ask an adult for help. Any parent who has ever been stuck with a last-minute project will be glad to help you plan. Any teacher who has ever heard long, boring excuses about why a project isn't done will be happy to help.

You wouldn't believe what happened. My dog chewed up my book...the library didn't have any extra copies...

Long-Term Project Planner

Assignment:_____ Date assigned: _____

Additions:_____

Additions:_____

How long will assignment and additions take to complete?

Steps to complete:	by when:
1.	
2.	
3.	
4.	
5.	
6.	

	Monday	Tuesday	Wednesday
Week 1			
Week 2			
Week 3			

te due: _____ **Number of days until due:** _____

_____ days

Notes:

ursday	Friday	Saturday	Sunday

Long-Term Project Planner

Assignment: Report on Civil War   Date assigned: Octobe

Additions: Maps, diagrams, pictures
Additions: Costume

How long will assignment and additions take to complete?

Steps to complete:	by when:
1. find books	October 5
2. take notes	October 9
3. make outline	Otober 11
4. write report	October 16
5. find maps, etc.	October 18
6. make costume	October 20

	Monday	Tuesday	Wednesday
Week 1	10/3 Get assignment	10/4 Search library	10/5 Search library
Week 2	10/10 Start outline	10/11 Finish outline	10/12 Write; work on cost
Week 3	10/17 Finish final draft	10/18 Finish maps	10/19 Costume

te due: <u>October 21</u> Number of days until due: <u>18</u>

<u>17</u> days

Notes:

the library closes early on Fridays

ursday	Friday	Saturday	Sunday
Take s; start me	10/7 Take notes	10/8 Take notes	10/9 Finish notes
3	10/14 Finish rough draft	10/15 Write final draft	10/16 Work on maps, etc.
) Finish me	10/21 Hand in report	Celebrate!	

Plan to Learn

You have the plan, you have the time—but do you have the **information** you need? A few simple strategies can help you organize your thoughts.

Take good class notes. For this, you'll need special note-taking paper. All it will cost is a little time—because you'll make it yourself, using regular lined paper, a ruler, and a red pencil.

About two inches from the left-hand side of the page, draw a **vertical** (up-and-down) **red line** down the whole length of the page. Do this on 10 pages (or more) and put them in the front of your binder.

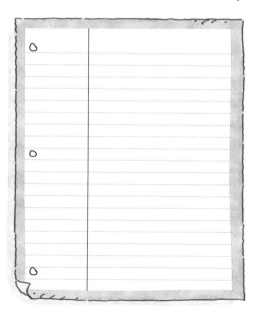

When you are listening to the teacher, use the wider **right-hand column** to write notes in short sentences. (Don't worry about grammar and punctuation. These notes are just for you.)

Use the narrower **left-hand column** to write key words—the most important words your teacher says. Like names of people and places, dates, and big ideas.

Middle Ages	From 5th century to 15th century
Visigoths	Germans who invaded Rome
Feudalism	Serfs worked on land but didn't own it

If your teacher **says** something like, "This is important," "Remember this," and especially (hello!) "This will be on the test," mark that note with a star.

If your teacher **writes** something on the board, add it to your notes.

If your teacher **repeats** something, add it to your notes.

Later, when you do your homework, go through your notes. Rewrite anything that is confusing or messy.* Make sure that you have written key words in the left-hand column. Add new key words to help you remember main ideas. Underline key words with colored pencils. Try grouping ideas by color.

You can also use this note-taking system when you're reading or studying on your own.

Two note-taking tips:

- **Skip lines between ideas.**
  That way, if you want to add more notes later to explain an idea, you'll have room.

- **Use only one side of the page.**
  Sometimes notes written on the backs of pages get "lost." You forget they're there.

* If there's something in your notes that's a total mystery, ask your teacher about it the next school day. Don't assume you'll figure it out when you need to—like the night before the test.

Use note cards and flash cards. Write key words and facts on note cards. Use flash cards to test your memory, especially in math and languages.

Tuck a few note cards and flash cards in your pocket or backpack. Peek at them during free moments (while waiting for the bus or waiting in line, for example).

Skim, highlight, read, summarize. Before you start reading a passage, **skim** it. Flip through the pages and read just the topic sentences (first sentences) of each paragraph. Look at the pictures and read the captions. What do you think is the main idea?

If the book belongs to you, **highlight** the key words. If it doesn't, write the key words on note cards.

Next, **read** the passage carefully. It should be easier to understand because you've already skimmed it. Finally, **summarize** what you read by writing it down in your notebook or on your note cards.

Pssst...

Every week or so, check your desk, locker, backpack, your homework place, and under your bed for library books. Look to see when they're due, and be sure to return them on time.

Library books are for everyone to use, so don't hog the ones you have. Keep them only as long as you need them. And take good care of them while you have them.

This goes for all school property, including your desk, your locker, and any textbooks. Those things don't really belong to you. You're just using them until the next person comes along.

Memory Tips and Tricks

Try these ideas for remembering things you need to know for quizzes, tests, or just because.

Turn a list of words into an acronym. An acronym uses the first letter of each word to make a new word. **Examples:** NBA is the acronym for National Basketball Association. SCUBA is the acronym for Self-Contained Underwater Breathing Apparatus.

PEMDAS could be your acronym for remembering the order of operations in math: Parentheses, Exponents, Multiplication, Division, Addition, Subtraction.

PEMDAS

Turn a list of words into a silly sentence. Do you need to remember the names of the planets in their order from the sun—Mercury, Venus, Earth, Mars, Jupiter, Saturn, Uranus, Neptune, Pluto? Make up a sentence using the first letters of each planet's name: "My Very Educated Mother Just Served Us Nine Pizzas."

For the organization of living things (kingdom, phylum, class, order, family, genus, species), try:

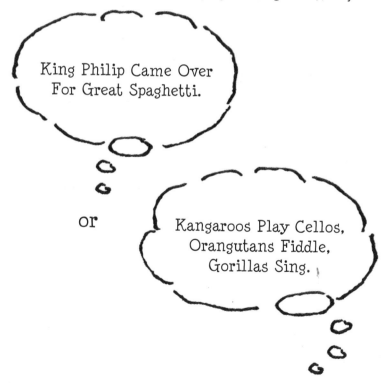

King Philip Came Over For Great Spaghetti.

or

Kangaroos Play Cellos, Orangutans Fiddle, Gorillas Sing.

Put a marble in your shoe. Do you have trouble remembering to bring your gym clothes to school on Tuesdays and Thursdays? Or do you forget your house key on Mondays and Fridays, when you have to let yourself in to your apartment after school? Sometimes it's hard to remember things that don't happen every day, or only happen once in a while.

Here's a way to remember occasional events. The night before, put a marble (or a stone, or something else small but hard) in your shoe. When you slip your foot into your shoe, you'll feel it, and your brain will go "AHA! There's something I need to remember!"

Talk it out. Say out loud what you're trying to learn. Instead of just **seeing** (reading), you'll also be **hearing** the sound of your voice and **feeling** your mouth make the words. The more senses you use while learning, the easier it is to remember what you learn.

Make up rhymes and songs. You probably learned the alphabet by singing the letters to the tune of "Twinkle, Twinkle, Little Star." Rhythm, repetition, rhyme, and melody can all help you remember things. "In fourteen-hundred-ninety-two, Columbus sailed the ocean blue...." "I before E except after C...." "Thirty days hath September...."

Chunk. You probably don't remember your phone number (or your friends' cell phone numbers) as long strings: 2125553982 or 4045551509. Instead, you mentally group them into smaller **chunks:** 212-555-3982, 404-555-1509. You can do this with any list of numbers—or even words. Try it and see.

Relate. Make a creative connection between old information and new information. **Example:** You already know that there's a country named Italy. Now you need to remember the name of an island close to that country—Sardinia. Imagine sardines on an Italian pizza.

Plan to Stay Organized Day-by-Day

Each morning, look at your planner. Are you ready for the day?

Before you leave home for school, make sure you have everything you need for the day. Backpack? Binder? Homework? Signed notes? Lunch? Special projects? What else?

At school, write your assignments on your homework checklist. Write due dates, quiz dates, and test dates in your planner.

Before you leave school for home, make sure you have everything you need for that night's homework. Handouts? Books? Worksheets? Notes? What else?

At home, stick to your homework schedule as closely as you can. Life happens, but try not to get off track too much.

Each night before you go to bed, look at your planner. Are you ready for tomorrow?

Each night before you go to bed, gather up everything you need for school the next day. Put it all in one place—on your desk, by the back door, or on the kitchen table. Try to use the same place every night.

Is It Worth It to Get Organized?

Maybe you're thinking, "Is it worth it to clean out my desk and locker and backpack and binder? Do I have to use a planner and fill out forms? Won't all that take a lot of time and effort?"

Sure it will—at first. But once you form the habit of being organized, it will take a lot **less** time and effort. And pretty soon you'll wonder why your desk was once a disaster, your locker was ever a shocker, and your backpack used to be a black hole.

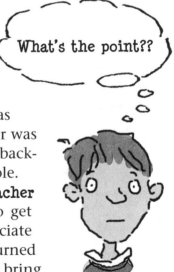

What's the point??

For one thing, **your teacher** will notice your efforts to get organized. Teachers appreciate tidy desks and neat work turned in on time. That can help bring up your grades.

Other kids at school will notice, too. They might compliment you for not being such a pigpen anymore. They might even ask you for pointers.

Your family will be grateful for the new, improved you. Who knows, some of your school habits could follow you home. Maybe you'll even start cleaning your room!

But most of all, you'll feel better about **yourself.** And you may have more free time than you ever imagined.

Experts say that disorganized people lose **one to two hours every day** looking for things, dealing with clutter, and procrastinating.

One to two hours every day times seven days a week equals seven to fourteen hours **every week.** That adds up to **hundreds** of hours every year.

Q: What will I do with that much extra time?

A: Whatever you want!

A Note
for Parents and Teachers

Today's school environment is highly competitive. Kids who can't find their homework, their planner, or a decent pencil are at risk for failure before they can even demonstrate their capabilities.

No parent wants a child to fail a test just because he forgot to write it down in his planner. No teacher wants to give a student a lower grade just because she forgot her homework.

If you're a parent who wants to help your child become more organized, here's how:

- Begin slowly. Focus on one problem at a time.

- Start with "stuff management." Filing papers properly and neatly arranging study tools on a desk can be done fairly quickly. The results are concrete and motivating.

- Shop for supplies with your child. Guide his choices. Find supplies that match his needs, the school's guidelines, and your pocketbook.

- Make sure that your child has a proper study space at home—one that's quiet, brightly lit, and prepared with tools and storage boxes.

- Work with your child to determine the best time to study. Study time should be roughly the same time each weekday.

- Make sure that your child studies or reads even when she has no assigned homework.

- See to it that your child has a proper backpack. Help him clean out his backpack each evening. Make sure that he reloads it, ready for school, at the end of study time.

- Spend time looking through your child's planner with your child. Show her how to use it. Check it each evening until she uses it consistently.

- Talk with your child's teacher. Get to know each other. A friendly, collaborative relationship will pay off handsomely for your child.

- Model organized behavior at home. Could you use some help? See pages 100–101.

If you're a teacher, try these ideas:

- Schedule a weekly classroom clean-up time. Encourage students to organize their desks and lockers, and have them file, trash, or take home loose papers.

- Permit responsible students to take home extra copies of heavy textbooks, if extras are available.

- Teach a lesson on planner use. Help students fill in planners daily. Check planners at the end of each day until students get the hang of it.

- If your students use homework folders, make sure they put homework in their folders instead of cramming it into their backpacks or desks.

- Provide interim deadlines for long-term projects. Even older students budget time poorly until they gain experience.

- Model organized behavior. Keep your desk tidy and your papers filed.

- Talk with the parents of kids who seem especially disorganized. It's possible that parents and other family adults are not modeling organized behavior at home. Lots of adults have problems with organization! You might refer parents to some of the helpful resources described on pages 100–101.

There's a fine line between helping kids get organized and doing it for them. The first teaches a life skill; the second reinforces dependency. With this in mind, both parents and teachers should:

- Keep expectations age-appropriate.

- Model appropriate choices, then allow independence.

- Permit kids to make mistakes without punishment. Reinforce that mistakes are learning opportunities.

- Allow for plenty of active fun time. Physical exercise is especially important for kids who tend to be disorganized.

Finally: Remember not to "lose it" yourself. Kids need to be kids, too! Which means that they will sometimes be messy, late, and disorganized. Try to be patient and don't expect perfection.

A few kids are born with a knack for organization. My own son wasn't one of them. It didn't happen overnight, but the strategies and techniques I taught him (and present in this book) are paying off. His grades have improved, his homework is usually on time, and he's a happy, independent, self-confident kid. What more could we parents and teachers ask?

Helpful Resources

For Kids

B. J. Pinchbeck's Homework Helper
school.discovery.com/homeworkhelp/bjpinchbeck/
Hundreds of links to homework help. More than 10,000 people visit each day.

Fact Monster
www.factmonster.com
An award-winning site packed with reference materials, homework help, fun facts, and cool stuff.

Organizing from the Inside Out for Teens: The Foolproof System for Organizing Your Room, Your Time, and Your Life by Julie Morgenstern and Jessi Morgenstern-Colón (New York: Henry Holt and Company, 2002). Julie wrote a bestselling book for grown-ups on getting organized. Here she teams up with her daughter, Jessi, to help busy teens make the most of their space and time.

Reaching Your Goals by Robin Landew Silverman (New York: Franklin Watts, 2004). To turn a wish into a goal takes creative thinking and organized planning skills. This book shows how to make a plan and see it through to the end.

School Power: Study Skill Strategies for Succeeding in School by Jeanne Shay Schumm, Ph.D. (Minneapolis: Free Spirit Publishing, 2001). Tips, strategies, charts, forms, and checklists help you read faster, study smarter, manage your time, keep track of assignments, do better on tests, and more.

Super Study Skills: The Ultimate Guide to Tests and Studying by Laurie Rozakis, Ph.D. (New York: Scholastic, 2002). How to get organized, prepare for tests without last-minute panic, study to get the grades you want, and more.

For Parents and Teachers

Homework Without Tears: A Parent's Guide for Motivating Children to Do Homework and to Succeed in School by Lee Canter and Lee Hausner, Ph.D. (New York: Harper and Row, 1999). This classic handbook helps parents deal with homework issues.

How to Double Your Child's Grades in School: Build Brilliance and Leadership in Your Child—from Kindergarten to College—in Just 5 Minutes Per Day by Eugene M. Schwartz (New York: Barnes & Noble Books, 2001). Describes simple methods designed to turn B's into A's, C's into B's, and help D students make significant improvements. The primary focus is on reading, writing, and arithmetic.

How to Help Your Child with Homework: The Complete Guide to Encouraging Good Study Habits and Ending the Homework Wars by Jeanne Shay Schumm, Ph.D. (Minneapolis: Free Spirit Publishing, 2005). How to set up a homework schedule and a home study center, help your child with projects, make peace at home, and more. Written by a teacher.

How to Organize Just About Everything: More Than 500 Step-by-Step Instructions for Everything from Organizing Your Closets to Planning a Wedding to Creating a Flawless Filing System by Peter Walsh (New York: Simon & Schuster, 2004). A professional organizer shares how-to instructions and tips to make every part of your life run more smoothly. A great guide to getting it all together.

A Mind at a Time: America's Top Learning Expert Shows How Every Child Can Succeed by Mel Levine, M.D. (New York: Simon & Schuster, 2002). Children have unique learning styles, and this book helps parents and teachers identify appropriate ways to teach to children as individuals. Visit Dr. Levine's Web site: allkindsofminds.org.

Organizing from the Inside Out: The Foolproof System for Organizing Your Home, Your Office, and Your Life by Julie Morgenstern (New York: Henry Holt and Company, 2004). Second edition. This *New York Times* bestseller has helped hundreds of thousands of people clean up the clutter in their life.

The Procrastinating Child: A Handbook for Adults to Help Children Stop Putting Things Off by Rita Emmett (New York: Walker, 2002). If you're driven to distraction by a child's procrastination, imagine how the child must feel. This book offers proven strategies and techniques for defusing friction, breaking through a child's defense mechanisms, and changing the procrastination habit.

Raising Happy Kids: Over 100 Tips for Parents and Teachers by Elizabeth Hartley-Brewer (Cambridge, MA: Da Capo Press, 2004). Practical advice for parents and teachers to help kids become self-reliant and successful. Also by the author: *Raising Confident Boys, Raising Confident Girls,* and *Raising a Self-Starter.*

Study Is Hard Work: The Most Accessible and Lucid Text Available on Acquiring and Keeping Study Skills Through a Lifetime by William H. Armstrong (Jaffrey, New Hampshire: David R. Godine, 1995). This still-in-print classic by the author of *Sounder* offers a common-sense approach to learning that adults and older students will find invaluable.

Index

About the Author

When Janet Fox was in third grade, her teacher, Mrs. Weber, sent a poem Janet had written to the town newspaper, and it was published. From that time on, Janet knew she would be a writer, and her joy at seeing her writing in print has never faded. The path to her profession wasn't straight. Along the way, she gained a husband, a son, a master's degree in geology, experience teaching high school English, a love of gardening, two dogs, a cat, and a horse. She grew up in New England, vacations in Montana, and currently resides in Texas.

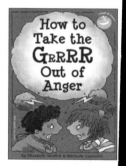